Choosing a Cat

How to Choose and Care for a Cat

Laura S. Jeffrey

THE AMERICAN HUMANE ASSOCIATION
Pet Care Series

Enslow Elementary
an imprint of
Enslow Publishers, Inc.
40 Industrial Road
Box 398
Berkeley Heights, NJ 07922
USA
http://www.enslow.com

American Humane Association™
The nation's voice for the protection of children & animals™

American Humane Association™
The nation's voice for the protection of children & animals™

Since 1877, American Humane Association has been at the forefront of virtually every major advance in protecting children, pets, and farm animals from cruelty, abuse, and neglect. Today we're also leading the way in understanding the human-animal bond and its role in therapy, medicine, and society. American Humane Association reaches millions of people every day through groundbreaking research, education, training, and services that span a wide network of organizations, agencies, and businesses. You can help make a difference, too. Visit www.americanhumane.org today, call 1-866-242-1877, or write to American Humane Association at 1400 16th Street NW, Suite 360, Washington, DC 20036.

To Our Readers: We have done our best to make sure all Internet addresses in this book were active and appropriate when we went to press. However, the author and the publisher have no control over and assume no liability for the material available on those Internet sites or on other Web sites they may link to. Any comments or suggestions can be sent by e-mail to comments@enslow.com or to the address on the back cover.

Every effort has been made to locate all copyright holders of material used in this book. If any errors or omissions have occurred, corrections will be made in future editions of this book.

♻ Enslow Publishers, Inc., is committed to printing our books on recycled paper. The paper in every book contains 10% to 30% post-consumer waste (PCW). The cover board on the outside of each book contains 100% PCW. Our goal is to do our part to help young people and the environment too!

Enslow Elementary, an imprint of Enslow Publishers, Inc.

Enslow Elementary® is a registered trademark of Enslow Publishers, Inc.

Copyright © 2013 by Enslow Publishers, Inc.

Library of Congress Cataloging-in-Publication Data
Jeffrey, Laura S.
  Choosing a cat : how to choose and care for a cat / Laura S. Jeffrey.
      p. cm. — (The american humane association pet care series)
  Includes bibliographical references and index.
  Summary: "Discusses the selection, housing, diet, handling, grooming, and health of a new cat"— Provided by publisher.
  ISBN 978-0-7660-4079-3
  1. Cats—Juvenile literature. I. Title.
  SF445.7.J457 2013
  636.8—dc23
                                        2011049132

Future Editions:
Paperback ISBN 978-1-4644-0214-2
ePUB ISBN 978-1-4645-1127-1
PDF ISBN 978-1-4646-1127-8

Printed in the United States of America

082012 Lake Book Manufacturing, Inc., Melrose Park, IL

10 9 8 7 6 5 4 3 2 1

Photo Credits: © 2012 Clipart.com, a division of Getty Images., p. 8; collasum/Photos.com, p. 37; Gregory Albertini/Photos.com, p. 16; GULCAN YASEMIN SUMER/Photos.com, p. 10; © iStockphoto.com/ Kim Gunkel, p. 19; © iStockphoto.com/Micah Young, p. 26; © iStockphoto.com/Shelly Perry, p. 32; Julia Pivovarova/Photos.com, p. 17; Kent Weakley/Photos.com, p. 9; Marek Tihelka/Photos.com, p. 22; Mark Chen/Photos.com, p. 30; Mark Hayes/Photos.com, p. 13; Shutterstock.com, pp. 1, 4, 5, 6, 7, 11, 12, 14, 15, 18, 20, 21, 23, 28, 29, 34, 35, 36, 38, 39, 40, 41, 42, 43, 44, 45; © Steve Pecoraro, p. 27; Troy Snow/Photos.com, pp. 24, 33.

Cover Photo: Shutterstock.com (gray tabby kitten)

Table of Contents

Chapter 1
Great Pets

Cats are beautiful, smart, and playful. They are fun to watch as they pounce on toys, swat at balls, and stretch after a long nap. Cats enjoy people as well as other cats, but they also like to be by themselves. They are easy to care for and easy to love. For all these reasons, cats are popular pets. Millions of Americans have at least one cat in their homes.

Cats are beautiful, smart, and playful.

This book will help you choose the right cat for you, whether it is a kitten or adult, a purebred or mixed-breed. It will tell you what kind of food to feed your new pet and how to make it feel comfortable and safe. You will learn how to keep your cat healthy and happy.

Fast Fact

Did you know cats can see better in dim light than people can?

Chapter 2

The History of Cats

The ancient Egyptians worshipped Bast, a goddess who took the form of a cat.

Long, long ago, cats were wild animals. But cats have been household pets for about four thousand years. The ancient Egyptians were the first to make cats household pets. They used cats to protect food supplies from rats and other pests. The ancient Egyptians thought of cats as gods and goddesses. They had laws against killing cats. People who killed cats could be put to death.

The History of Cats

Ancient Egyptians drew pictures of cats on walls. They were the first to have cats as pets.

By the 1700s, people all over the world had cats as pets. Cats came to America with the Pilgrims, who used cats on the *Mayflower* and other ships to hunt rats. Cats became more than just workers. They became friends.

Today, there are more than forty different breeds of cats. Cats can be purebreds, meaning they are just one breed of cat, or they can be mixed-breeds. Some are solid colored. Others have color patterns, such as stripes, spots, or patches. Cats may have short hair or long hair, smooth coats or even curly coats. Some cats have long, fluffy tails, while others have short, stubby tails. Some cats have ears that fold down, while others have ears that stand up.

There are many different breeds of cats all over the world.
This is a Persian cat.

Siamese cats are just one type of breed.

For purebred cats, the American shorthair is a popular cat breed. This breed is known for its beauty and gentle nature. American shorthairs get along well with children and dogs. They come in about eighty different colors and patterns. The most common American shorthair is silver with black markings.

Siamese cats come from Thailand, which was once called Siam. Siamese cats have short, light-colored coats. They have darker blue, brown, lilac, lynx (striped), or red markings on their legs, tails, ears, and faces. Siamese cats like to sit in their owner's lap. Some people think the purring of a Siamese cat sounds like singing.

Cats can live for an average of ten to fifteen years. With proper care, they will give their owners love and friendship for many years.

Fast Fact

Today there are many cultures that believe cats bring good luck. In Japan, people decorate their homes with ceramic cat sculptures.

Chapter 3
The Right Cat for You

What kind of cat is best for you? First, you should decide whether you want a cat or a kitten. Kittens are adorable and fun to play with. But a kitten is a friend and playmate, not a toy. If you have a younger brother or sister, you probably should get a cat instead of a kitten. Your little brother or sister may accidentally hurt a little kitten. Adult cats can be playful and silly, too. They may also get into less trouble.

Before deciding which cat you would like, you have to think about whether you want a kitten or a cat.

Another decision is what breed of cat to get. Some cat breeds are better for children and families. You can learn about the different breeds of cats through the Internet or library books.

If the adults in your house agree, you may want to adopt two cats instead of just one. Most cats enjoy company. They also like to have fun late at night. Having two cats means there will always be a playmate for the other one.

Fast  Fact

Cats can use sound, body signals, and scents to communicate. An arched back means fear or anger.

Where Will You Get Your New Pet?

Your first stop should be your local animal shelter. There, you will find many healthy, adorable, and loving cats and kittens in need of a home. Most of the cats and kittens in the shelter will probably be mixed-breeds.

Workers at the shelter have gotten to know these animals. They will help match you with the right pet for your family. Also, adopting a pet is the best way to help animals.

Local animal shelters charge a small fee to adopt a pet.
This money helps the other homeless animals in the shelter.

Kittens are cute and fun to watch. But adult cats are just as playful as kittens. Many older cats need homes.

The Right Cat for You

If you want a certain type of cat that is not currently available at the shelter, ask shelter workers about a breed-placement group. This is a group of concerned people who take in unwanted cats and find homes for them. You can also buy a cat or kitten from a breeder. However, breeders may charge a lot of money.

The American Humane Association says people should not get a cat from a pet store. Pet stores are not as concerned about matching people with a pet that will fit well into their lifestyle.

Getting a purebred cat does not always have to be expensive. Some rescue groups only deal with one breed.

Chapter 4

Taking Care of Your Cat

You probably cannot wait to spend time holding and playing with your new cat. But you need to give it plenty of time to get to know its new home. You also need to give it time to get to know you. When you first bring your cat home, keep it in one room. The cat will feel more secure if it learns its way around one room at a time. Let it slowly explore its new home.

18

Be sure to give your new cat time to get to know you and its new home.

Taking Care of Your Cat

Slowly and quietly let it meet other family members and household pets. In time, cats adapt happily to any house or apartment. They never need to go outside, where cars, diseases, other cats, dogs, and bad people can harm them.

Eating

Always have a bowl of fresh, cool drinking water for your cat. Do not give your cat milk because it may cause diarrhea. Feed your cat a high-quality, brand-name food made for cats. The three main types are dry, soft-moist, and canned. Ask your veterinarian what kind of food is best for your cat and how much food to feed it. Always feed your cat in the same place and at the same time. Do not touch or bother your cat while it is eating.

Some kittens might be too young to adopt. Ask your local animal shelter if a kitten is ready to be adopted. Small kittens need to be fed special formula with a bottle.

Taking Care of Your Cat

Do not feed your cat human food because it may not have the right kinds of nutrients your pet needs. Also, cats should never be fed bones or raw fish.

Kittens should stay with their mothers until they are at least eight weeks old so they can drink their mother's milk. If you adopt a kitten younger than this, ask a veterinarian how to feed it.

Just like people, cats need a well-balanced diet. And always have a bowl of fresh water out for your cat.

Cats like to sleep a lot! They like cozy places like their own beds, but they may find their own special places to sleep.

Sleeping

Cats take plenty of long naps. They like to sleep in a padded, shallow box or basket. They may also end up choosing their own resting place, such as your bed or a sunny windowsill. Cats may sleep as much as eighteen hours a day.

Using the Litter Box

The best toilet for your cat is a plastic litter pan, or litter box. Cover the bottom of the pan with about two inches of litter. Clumping cat litter is easier to scoop than regular litter. Put the pan someplace where your cat will not be bothered or annoyed by other pets or household activity. Make sure the pan is far away from the cat's food and water bowls.

Cats use a litter box as a bathroom. Some litter boxes are pans with no tops. Others, like this one, are enclosed.

Name
Phone No.

In case your cat gets lost, a tag on a collar has the contact information to get your cat returned to you.

Your cat will naturally want to use the pan, so you should not have to worry about training it. Just make sure your cat knows where the pan is. In a two-story house, you might need one pan upstairs and another one downstairs. A very young kitten may need a few litter pans at first.

Keep the litter pan clean. Otherwise, your cat may decide to use the corner of a room instead. Scoop out the waste at least once a day. Change the litter and wash the box with a mild soap as often as needed.

Identification

Buy your cat a collar that has an elastic insert. If your cat gets caught on something, the elastic in the collar will expand so the cat can free itself without getting hurt.

On the collar, place an identification (ID) tag with your family's name, address, and phone number on it. Even a house cat might slip through an open door or window and become lost. An identification tag lets neighbors or animal shelter workers return your pet to you. Also, ask the adults you live with to find out if you need a city or county license for your cat.

Pet  Pointer

The microchip is about the size of a grain of rice and is put under the skin. Even if your cat is microchipped, it should still wear a tag and collar with its name and your family's address on it.

A microchip is a very small computer chip. More and more people are having vets put microchip IDs into their cats. This is a safe and effective way to have a permanent ID for your cat. However, some people who find cats do not know that they may have a microchip. So it is a good idea to have an identification tag on your pet's collar at all times. That way, you will help your pet find its way home if it ever becomes lost.

In case your pet gets outside accidentally and becomes lost, or in case of an emergency, such as a fire or flood, have information about your pet ready to share. This includes a recent photo, vaccination records, vet information, and names and phone numbers to contact.

Grooming

You will not need to bathe your pet because cats clean themselves with their very rough tongues. But some cats do enjoy baths. If you give your cat a bath, use warm water and soap made for cats. Do not use a shampoo used for dogs because it could harm your cat. Let your cat dry off in a warm place.

Even though you will not have to bathe your cat often, you should regularly brush its coat. Brushing helps prevent hair balls. When cats lick their coats to clean themselves, they swallow pieces of hair.

If you have to bathe your cat, be careful not to get water in its ears or soap in its eyes.

Fast Fact

Cats clean themselves with their very rough tongues.

The hair forms a ball in the cat's stomach. Sometimes, cats throw up hair balls. Regular combing can help prevent hair balls from forming. Long-haired cats should be combed daily with a steel comb. A brush works well on short-haired cats.

You can also buy a paste to feed your cat as a treat. The paste will help the cat pass the hair through its body instead of throwing it up as a hair ball.

Praising

Most cats love attention. Make sure you talk to your pet. Praise or say good things to your cat when it is good, and include it in your day-to-day activities, when possible. Remember that your gentle words and behavior will make your cat even more loving.

Chapter 5

Healthy and Happy

A veterinarian, often called a vet, is a doctor who takes care of sick and hurt animals. A vet also makes sure animals stay healthy. Soon after you bring your cat home, make an appointment with a vet. The vet will examine your cat and make sure it is healthy. The vet also will schedule the shots your new pet needs to protect it from diseases. One of these diseases is rabies. If a cat with rabies bites or scratches you, then you could get rabies, too.

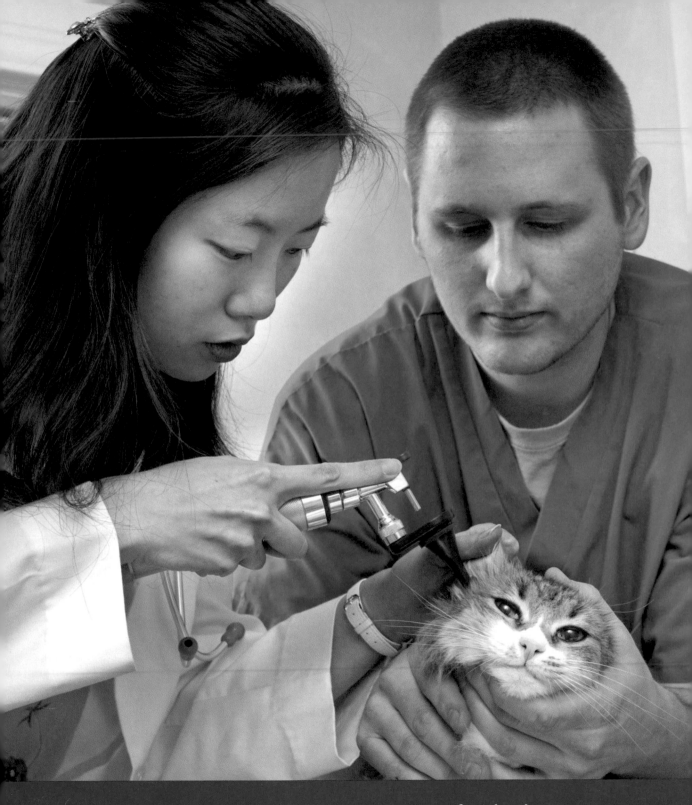

Be sure to take your pet to a vet for checkups.

Other health concerns for cats are intestinal parasites and heartworm. Also, cats are more likely than dogs to catch diseases that cause breathing trouble.

Ask your veterinarian how you can tell when your cat is sick. For example, cats have a third eyelid, called the nictitating (nik-te-tate-ing) membrane. This third eyelid sometimes can be seen when a cat gets sick. Also, cats that are sick may stop using their litter box. They go to the bathroom in other areas of the house.

Also ask your vet about how to get help if there is an emergency after the vet's regular office hours. That way, you will know when and how to get help for your pet.

Spaying and Neutering

The vet will want to talk to you and the adults you live with about getting your cat spayed, if it is a female, or neutered, if it is a male. To spay or neuter is to operate on an animal so it cannot reproduce. Spaying and neutering prevent overpopulation. Every year, millions of lovable cats and kittens must be euthanized, or put to death, in animal shelters because there are no homes for them.

Spaying or neutering your cat is helpful. Behavioral problems will lessen, and your cat may even become more loving.

Fast  Fact

There are not enough homes for all the cats alive today, so do not let your cat have kittens.

If your cat is eight weeks or older, it is old enough to be spayed or neutered. Most animals in local shelters are spayed or neutered before they are put up for adoption.

Spaying and neutering are safe operations. Also, the operation may be helpful to your cat. Neutered males lose their urge to roam and fight with other cats. Cats are less likely to spray where they should not. They usually become calmer and more loving. Another advantage to spaying and neutering is that it will prevent your cat from getting certain diseases.

Playing

To make sure your cat stays healthy, play with your cat. Playing is how cats get their exercise. You can buy toys for your cat at a pet supply store or use objects around the house. Cats love things that they can chase, pull, or swat.

Cats like to play. Give them toys that are safe for them, like this ball.

They like small, round objects, such as Ping-Pong balls and golf balls. They enjoy playing with wadded-up paper and in boxes. Cats also like to climb into paper bags. Remember that plastic bags can be dangerous for cats, just as they are dangerous for humans.

Chapter 6

Preventing Problems

Cats are smart. Your pet can be trained to come when its name is called. It can also learn to stop doing something when you say "no." Some cats can perform tricks. They can also be trained to use the toilet instead of a litter box.

But cats are not as easy to train as dogs are. If you try to train your cat, remain calm and keep doing the same thing. Like dogs, cats respond to food rewards and attention. They will not change their behavior if you punish them, so you should never hit a cat.

Scratching

Scratching is one cat behavior that humans find annoying. But for cats, scratching is normal and necessary behavior. You need to have a place where your cat can scratch, or it will find its own place. Your pet could tear up carpeting or furniture with its claws.

To prevent problems, you should get your cat a few scratching posts. Put them in different areas of the house your cat can easily get to. You can buy them at a pet supply store. Or you can make them with a special rope called sisal. Some cats like horizontal (across) scratching surfaces. Others prefer vertical (up-and-down) ones.

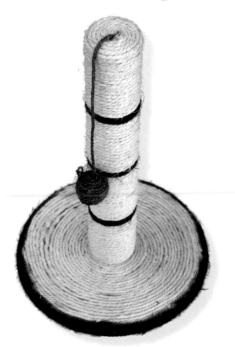

Avoid scratching posts with carpeting because this might confuse cats. They may think it is okay to scratch any carpeting in the house.

Cats like to scratch. Buying your pet a few special scratching posts will save your curtains and furniture.

36

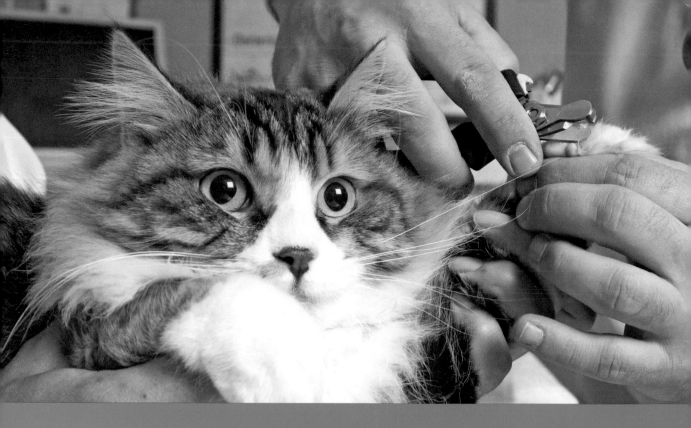

Trim your cat's nails to protect you from scratches.

Cover places in the house that you want to protect from scratching with thick plastic. Your cat will learn to avoid these places. Then, you can safely remove the plastic.

Some veterinarians declaw cats to prevent them from scratching. Many animal experts say that declawing is cruel. Instead, trim your cat's nails to protect you and your furniture from scratches. A vet can show you how to give your cat a proper manicure. If you cut the nails too short, you could hit a bundle of nerves called the quick.

Some household plants are poisonous to cats. Be sure plants are kept away from where a cat can get to them. You can grow special grasses just for your cat.

Keeping Out of Trouble

Cats are very curious, but their curiosity can get them into trouble. The best solution is to remove items that cats will want to check out. Keep food off the kitchen counter. Place houseplants and fishbowls out of your cat's reach. Make sure such items as household cleaners, medicine, makeup, and needles and thread are safely put away.

Cats like to climb and jump. You can buy a cat tree for your cat to play on. They come in many different sizes.

Preventing Problems

Also, remember to close the clothes dryer door. If left open, a cat may climb inside to bask in the warmth after a load of clothes has been removed. But your pet may be overlooked when the next load of clothes is thrown in.

Cats like spending time in high places where they can keep an eye on people and other pets. Keep windowsills and the tops of tall furniture empty so your cat will have a safe place to hang out. Be aware that cats can climb to the highest and most dangerous shelf in the house.

Keep windowsills empty so your cat can enjoy the outside view.

Pet 🐭 Pointer

Keeping the house vacuumed and brushing your cat daily are two ways to make life easier for people allergic to cats.

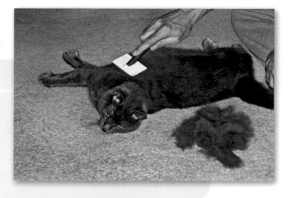

Cats also can pull open cabinet drawers unless the drawers are secured in some way. Also, many cats can squeeze through small openings in windows and doors. Be sure that window screens are secure, especially the windows on high floors.

Allergies

Sometimes, people bring a cat home and then discover they are allergic to it. Actually, they are allergic to the cat's dander. Dander is the tiny flakes of dried skin or hair on a cat's skin. People who are allergic to cats sneeze or get itchy eyes and skin rashes when they get near cats.

You can buy special sprays for a cat's coat to lessen the amount of dander. You can also take medicine to prevent allergic reactions.

Chapter 7
You and Your New Cat

After you bring a cat into your home, you will be happy to spend time with it.

You can find more information about cats at a library or on the Internet. Ask an adult to help you.

Remember that cats can live to be fifteen or more years old. Keep loving and learning more about your pet, and you and your cat will spend many happy years together.

Have fun playing with and loving your pet for many years.

Life Cycle of a Cat

1. A newborn kitten has no teeth and its eyes are closed. After several days, a kitten will open its eyes. All kittens' eyes are blue.

2. After several months, a cat's eyes will change to their permanent color. Cats are fully grown by the time they are one year old.

3. Cats stay playful for most of their lives. With proper care, they can live up to fifteen years or longer.

Words to Know

breed—To control when an animal reproduces; a group of animals with similar features.

dander—Tiny bits from skin or hair that may cause allergies.

microchip—A very small computer chip put inside an animal as an identification tag.

mixed-breed—Having features from more than one breed of animal.

neuter—To perform an operation so a male animal cannot reproduce.

purebred—Belonging to a breed with the same features through many generations of animals.

quick—A very sensitive area underneath a nail.

sisal—A strong fiber used to make rope and other items.

spay—To perform an operation so a female animal cannot reproduce.

Read More About Cats

Books

Armentrout, David, and Patricia Armentrout. *Kitty Care.* Vero Beach, Fla.: Rourke Pub., 2011.

Johnson, Jinny. *Cats and Kittens.* Mankato, Minn.: Smart Apple Media, 2009.

Wilsdon, Christina. *Cats.* Pleasantville, N.Y.: Gareth Stevens Pub., 2009.

Internet Addresses

American Humane Association
<http://www.americanhumane.org/>

Animal Planet: Pets 101
<http://animal.discovery.com/petsource/>

Index